ANGRY BIRDS™

Amigurumi
and more

Content and patterns by Elina Hiltunen
Pattern testing and yarns by Novita Oy, www.novita.fi
Tutorial videos on www.youtube.com/novitatube

Editing by Juha Kallio & Rovio Books
Translation by Owen F. Witesman
Photographs by Minna Kurjenluoma
Cover design and layout by Terhi Haikonen

Translation rights arranged by Elina Ahlback Literary Agency

ISBN 978-1-58923-870-1
Printed in China

ANGRY BIRDS™
Amigurumi
and more

ARTS & CRAFTS

Contents

7   INTRODUCTION

9   THE BASICS OF AMIGURUMI

10   STITCHES AND STARTS

16   OTHER CROCHETING TIPS

19   INSTRUCTIONS FOR MAKING CHARACTERS

23   **CROCHETING ANGRY BIRD CHARACTERS**

25   RED

28   BOMB

33   MATILDA

37   CHUCK

40   JIM AND JAKE AND JAY

44   THE EGGS

47   KING PIG

52   CORPORAL PIG

57   MINION PIG

60   WOOD, STONE, AND ICE BLOCKS

62   SLINGSHOT

66   LET THE GAMES BEGIN!

69   **CROCHET YOURSELF SOME BIRD-WEAR!**

71   SILLY SNOUT HAT

77   RICOCHET CROCHET CAP

82   BLASTING CAP

87   BLUE LIGHTNING PHONE PURSE

90   PIGGY-PROOF TABLET CASE

INTRODUCTION

You've probably played Angry Birds. You're not alone! There are millions of players and fans just like you (and me!) all over the world. The Angry Birds and Bad Piggies have conquered every continent and even gone into space.

Craft people have gotten into the act too, making all sorts of amazing bird and pig creations. Online blogs are filled to overflowing with designs from enthusiastic crafters, crocheters, knitters, and sewers based on the Angry Birds world.

Lots of people have asked me for advice on making Angry Birds amigurumi, which are crocheted or knitted stuffed figures. How do you crochet Red glowing with rage or Bomb bursting at his seams?

In this book, you will find instructions for making the whole flock of birds and a passel of pigs. Use them to make all your favorite Angry Birds characters, the wood, stone, and ice blocks from the game, and even the slingshot. You can crochet the entire Angry Birds game! And you really can use them to play the game.

Why stop there? Make Angry Birds caps or a purse or a tablet case featuring your favorite characters. A word of warning is in order though: crocheting Angry Birds characters is as addictive as playing the game!

Elina

Elina Hiltunen, M.Sc., D.Sc., and futurist. In addition to her regular job, Elina designs crochet patterns for Novita, the largest yarn company in Finland, and has previously written a guide on the ABC's of amigurumi crocheting.

THE BASICS OF AMIGURUMI

Before you can start making Angry Birds characters, you need to review the basics of crocheting amigurumi. Of course, the basic supplies for crocheting always include a crochet hook and yarn.

Crochet hooks come in different sizes, and the systems for measuring them can be confusing. These days most hooks list a size in millimeters on the packaging. The bigger the millimeter size, the thicker the hook and the heavier the yarn you crochet with it.

The thickness of hook to use depends both on the yarn and the hand technique of the person doing the crocheting. The labeling on a ball of yarn recommends what size of crochet hook to use with it.

When crocheting amigurumi, it's a good idea to use a crochet hook that will give you a tight surface so the stuffing doesn't show through. One thing to try is using a hook 0.5 mm smaller than the size recommended on the yarn packaging. So if the yarn recommends using hook number 4 (in millimeters), first see what kind of results you get with a 3.5. Make sure you're looking at the millimeter sizes though, because in some other sizing systems, bigger numbers mean thinner hooks!

For crocheting your Angry Birds characters, you can use different kinds and weights of yarn. Remember though that if you crochet the same pattern using lighter or heavier yarn, the characters will end up different sizes. Heavier yarn will give you bigger figures, and lighter yarn will give you smaller figures. Because not all the Angry Birds characters are the same size, all of the patterns in this book use the same weight of yarn. The figures in the book were designed using Novita 7 Veljestä yarn, which recommends a 4 mm crochet hook. A 3.5 mm hook was actually used to crochet them though.

STITCHES AND STARTS

Crocheting amigurumi is actually quite easy, because you mostly just use one kind of stitch: the single crochet (called double crochet in the United Kingdom). In addition to this stitch, you also need to know the loop stitch, chain stitch, how to increase and decrease stitches, and how to change colors. All of these different stitches and stages of work are covered on the following pages.

SLIPKNOT

Starting a chain stitch begins with a slipknot. To make a slipknot:

1. Wind yarn around finger.
2. Hook the yarn under the yarn wrapped around your finger.
3. Pull tight.

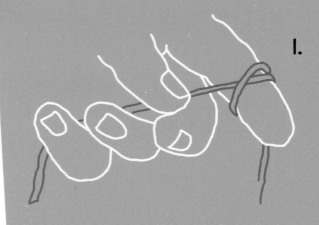

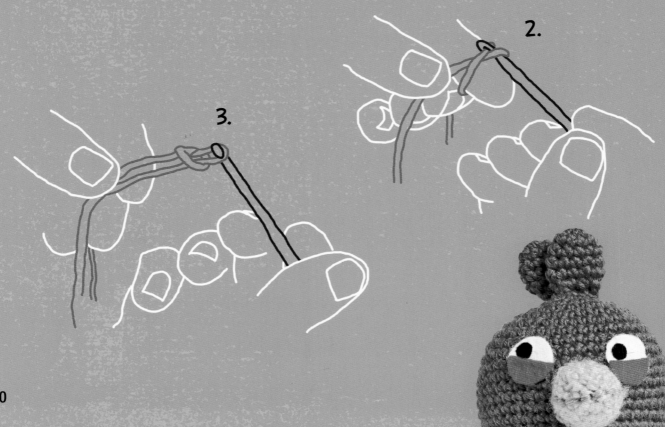

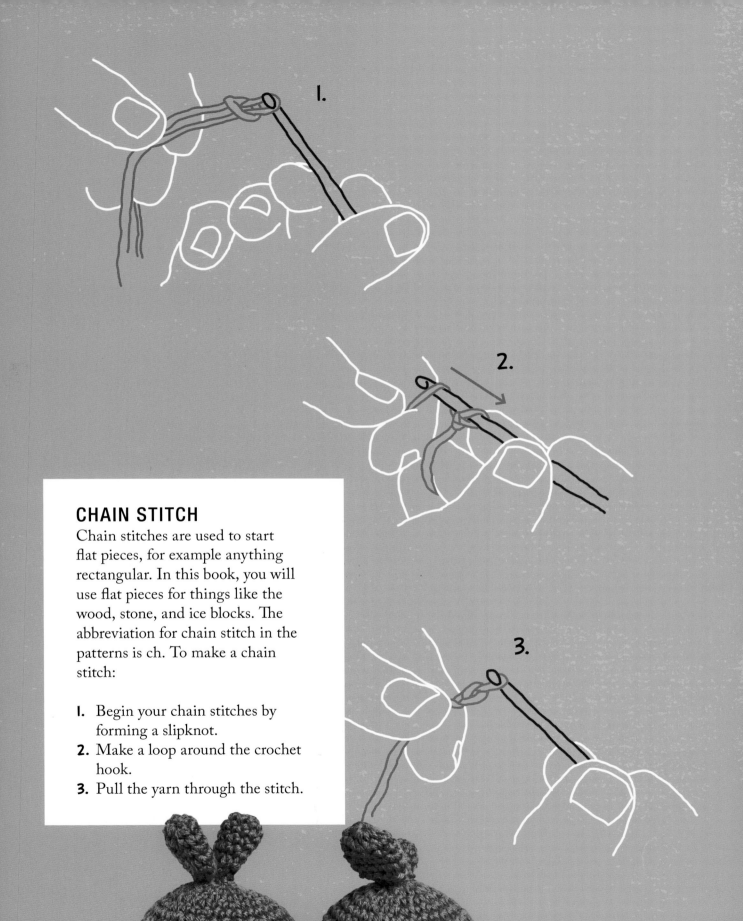

CHAIN STITCH

Chain stitches are used to start flat pieces, for example anything rectangular. In this book, you will use flat pieces for things like the wood, stone, and ice blocks. The abbreviation for chain stitch in the patterns is ch. To make a chain stitch:

1. Begin your chain stitches by forming a slipknot.
2. Make a loop around the crochet hook.
3. Pull the yarn through the stitch.

SLIP STITCH

The slip stitch is meant to be kept out of sight. Uses for it include inconspicuously linking the first and last stitches of a round in a circle. The abbreviation for the slip stitch in the patterns is sl st. To make it:

1. Insert hook through a stitch in the previous round.
2. Make a loop around the hook.
3. Pull the yarn through all of the loops on the hook.

SINGLE CROCHET

The single crochet is the basic stitch for making amigurumi. In the patterns, a single crochet is indicated by the abbreviation sc. To do the single crochet stitch:

1. Insert hook through a stitch in the previous round.
2. Make a loop around the hook.
3. Draw the hook and yarn through the stitch in the previous round. Two loops will be left on the hook.
4. Make a loop around the hook.
5. Pull the yarn through the loops on the hook.

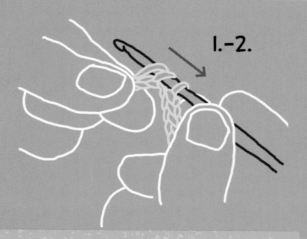

1.–2.

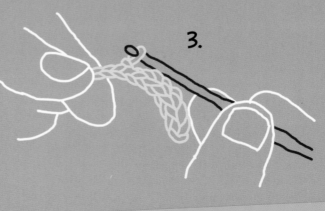

3.

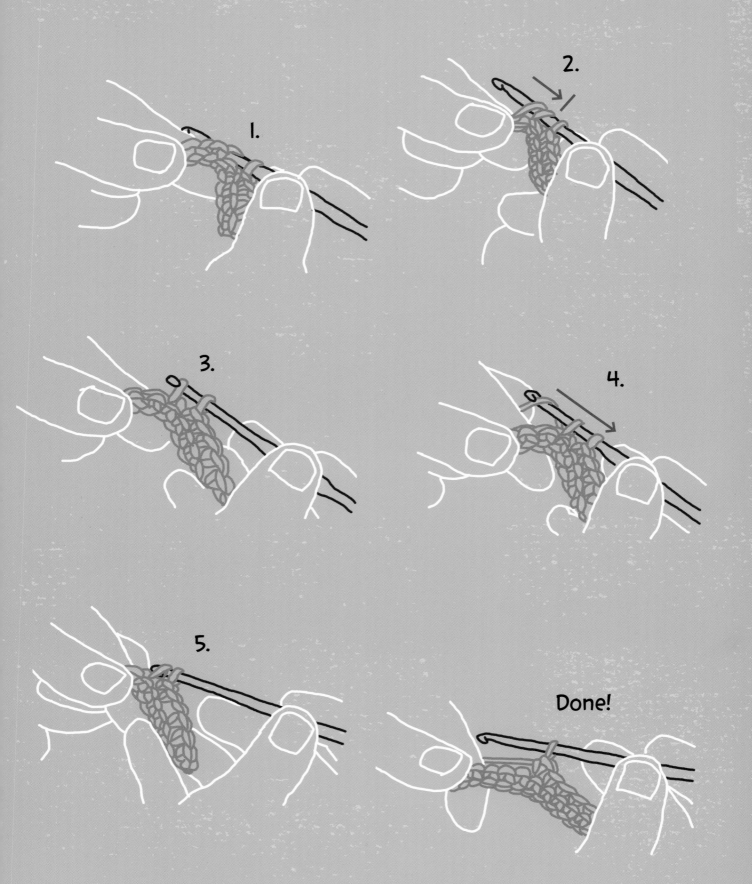

1.

2.

3.

4.

5.

Done!

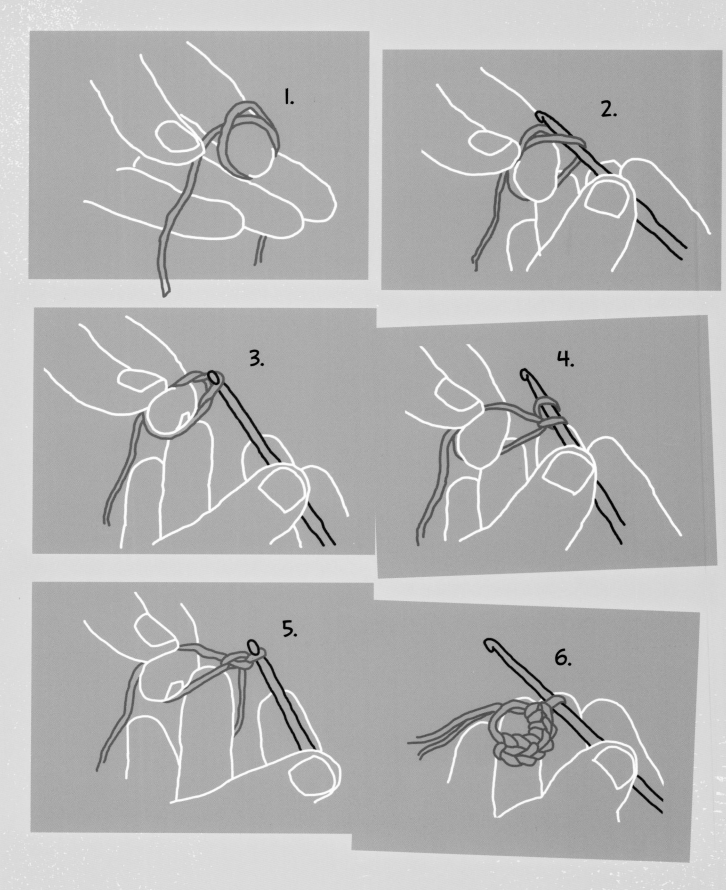

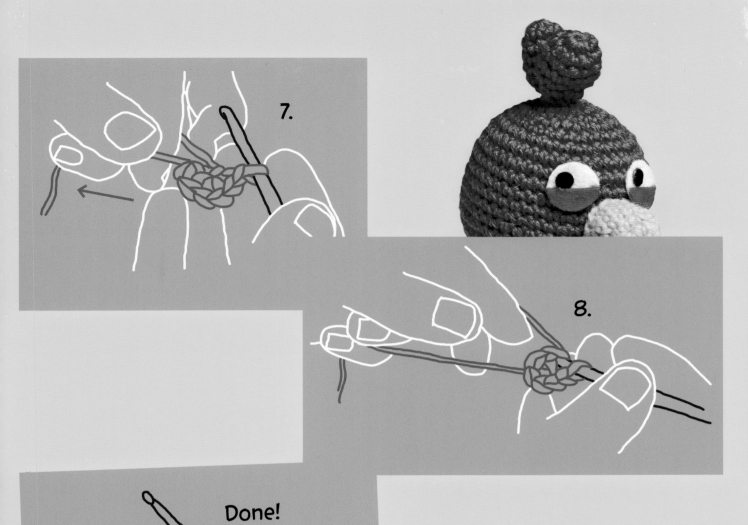

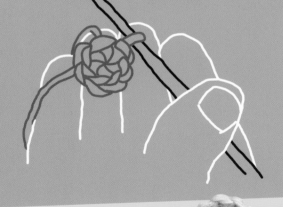

7.

8.

Done!

CENTER RING START

Crocheting round objects, like birds and pigs, always begins with a center ring. To make a center ring:

1. Wind yarn around finger.
2.–6. Make the necessary number of single crochet stitches for the ring.
7. Tighten the ring by pulling the short end of the yarn.
8. You can also fasten the stitches into a ring using a slip stitch.

OTHER CROCHETING TIPS

INCREASING AND DECREASING

Increasing stitches and decreasing stitches is how to make three-dimensional characters.

Increasing means crocheting two single crochet stitches into one stitch in the previous round. In the patterns, increasing is indicated as follows: 2 sc in next st.

When decreasing, we crochet one stitch into two stitches from the previous round. In the patterns, decreasing is indicate as follows: sc2tog, which means working one single crochet in each two stitches of the previous row.

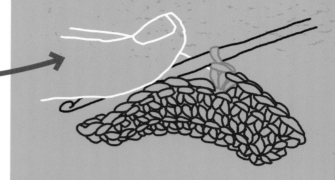

1.

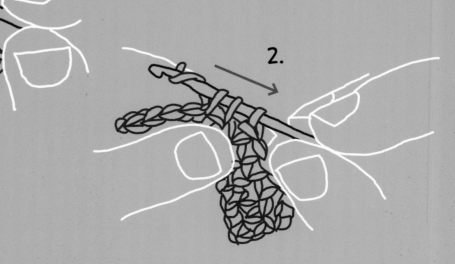

2.

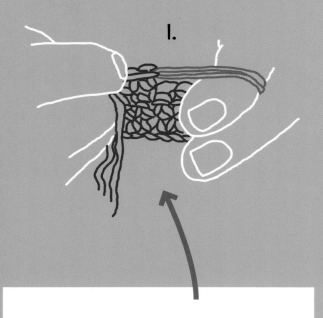

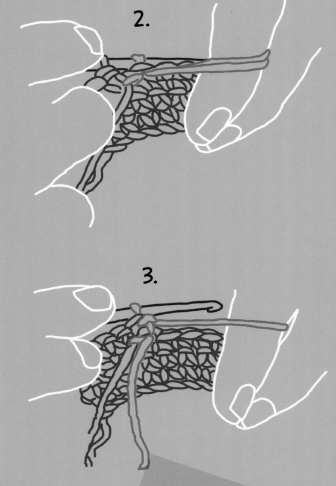

CHANGING YARN COLOR

If the color of the yarn changes periodically (like in Bomb's crest), the new yarn is wrapped around the old on the back of the piece. The ends of the yarn are tied off so they won't come undone. When the yarn changes, the last step of the last single crochet stitch of the old yarn is made with the new yarn.

CHANGING ROWS AND ROUNDS

When crocheting flat pieces (like rectangles), the piece is turned at the end of each row. When you turn the work, you always make a turning chain so the edges of the work stay even. When single crocheting, the turning chain is one chain stitch.

The method used in this book for crocheting circles and balls calls for making the rounds (rows) in a spiral. This means that the rounds are not finished off separately—crocheting continues uninterrupted from one round to the next. Another way to crochet a circle or a ball is to close off each round with a slip stitch and then crochet a turning chain at the beginning of the new row.

READING THE PATTERNS
The patterns in this book use the following abbreviations:

rnd	round
st	stitch
sc	single crochet
sl st	slip stitch
ch	chain stitch
sc2tog	single crochet two stitches together (decrease)
-	Repeat instruction between stars (as many times as indicated).

Each Angry Birds character pattern proceeds round by round. Below is an excerpt from Bomb's pattern, showing what the different parts of the pattern mean.

Center Ring Start

Increasing

Decreasing

BODY, BLACK – CROCHETED FROM BOTTOM TO TOP
Wrap black yarn once around finger and then work onto the resulting loop:

Rnd 1: Sc 10. Work round in a spiral, moving directly to the next row.

Rnd 2: 2 sc in each st = 20 sc.

Rnd 3: Sc 20.

Rnd 4: *Sc 1, 2 sc in next st*, repeat 10 times = 30 sc.

Rnd 5-6: Sc 30.

Rnd 7: *Sc 1, 2 sc in next st*, repeat 15 times = 45 sc.

Rnd 8: Sc 45.

Rnd 9: *Sc 2, 2 sc in next st*, repeat 15 times = 60 sc.

Rnd 10: Sc 60.

Rnd 11: *Sc 5, 2 sc in next st*, repeat 10 times = 70 sc.

Rnd 12-26: Sc 70.

Rnd 27-30: *Sc 1, sc2tog*, repeat over 4 rounds, leaving a hole.

INSTRUCTIONS FOR MAKING CHARACTERS

SUPPLIES

In addition to yarn and a crochet hook, you will need a few basic supplies for making your birds and pigs. To make the characters in this book, you will also need the following items: craft felt, glue, stuffing, beads, sharp scissors, a darning needle, and a sewing needle. You can get these supplies from a craft store or through the Internet.

For making the slingshot, you'll need some plywood and a jigsaw to cut a piece the right shape out of the plywood. You can get these supplies from a hardware store. Each pattern includes a detailed list of materials.

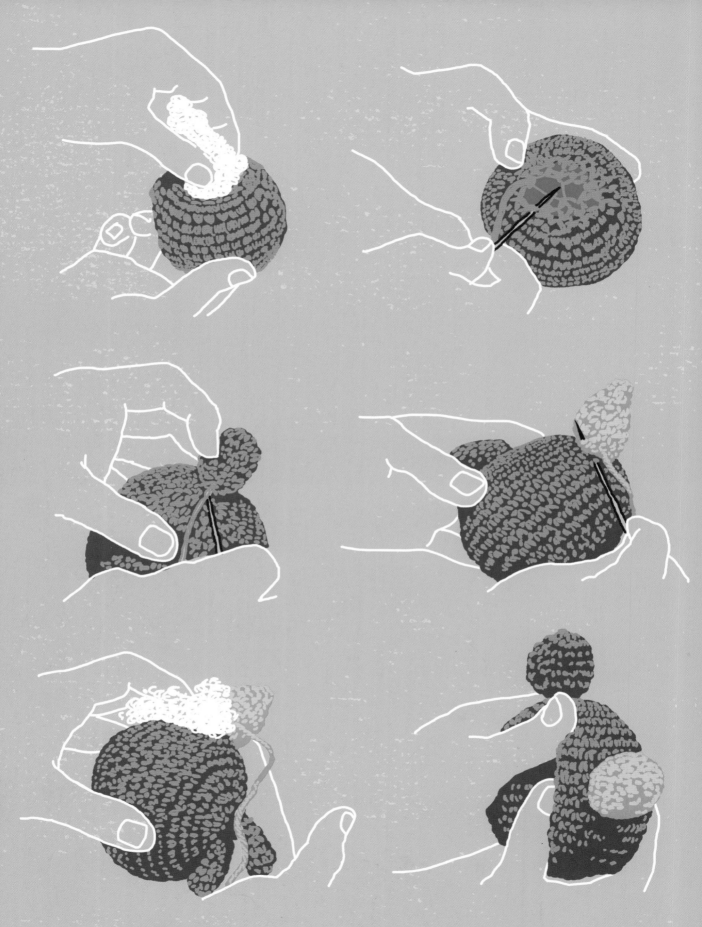

CHARACTER ASSEMBLY

You assemble your Angry Birds characters out of different parts (e.g. beak, breast patch, crests), some of which are stuffed. Once you've finished crocheting a piece, cut the yarn, but leave it long enough for connecting other pieces. Sew the pieces together with a darning needle and finish off.

The best material for stuffing the characters is polyester batting, which you can buy from a craft or sewing store. You can also salvage stuffing from pillows for your amigurumi. Each character is stuffed through a hole you leave while crocheting and then sew shut with a darning needle after stuffing. Spending some time arranging the stuffing in the figure is a good idea to get it just the right shape. You can also cover the stuffing with fabric the same color as the yarn around the hole before sewing it shut. That way the white fibers aren't as visible through the stitching.

SEWING TIPS

A handy way to give the birds' beaks an upper and lower half is by sewing a line across it with a darning needle. Doing this sewing you use two different stitches: the backstitch and the chain stitch.

CROCHETING ANGRY BIRDS CHARACTERS

In the next section, we get down to the actual work of crocheting the birds, pigs, eggs, and blocks, not to mention the birds' propulsion device, the slingshot. Once you've finished a few characters and the slingshot, you can try out how well a crocheted Angry Birds game works!

RED

Red is the leader of the Angry Birds and the angriest bird of all. He isn't the strongest, but his bird brain power is beak and feathers above the rest. In his position, Red feels the weight of responsibility and spends all his time watching over the flock and their eggs.

- Yarn: lightweight smooth red, beige, and yellow
- Crochet hook
- Felt: white, black, and burgundy
- Stuffing

BODY, RED – CROCHETED FROM TOP TO BOTTOM.

Wrap red yarn once around finger and then work onto the resulting loop:

Rnd 1: Sc 10. Work round in a spiral, moving directly to the next row.

Rnd 2: 2 sc in each st = 20 sc.

Rnd 3: Sc 20.

Rnd 4: *Sc 1, 2 sc in next st*, repeat 10 times = 30 sc.

Rnd 5: Sc 30.

Rnd 6: Sc 30.

Rnd 7: *Sc 1, 2 sc in next st*, repeat 15 times = 45 sc.

Rnd 8: Sc 45.

Rnd 9: *Sc 2, 2 sc in next st*, repeat 15 times = 60 sc.

Rnd 10-17: Sc 60.

→

Rnd 18: *Sc 2, sc2tog*, repeat 15 times = 45 sc.

Rnd 19-20: Sc 45.

Rnd 21: *Sc 1, sc2tog*, repeat 15 times = 30 sc.

Rnd 22: Sc 30.

Rnd 23 on: *Sc 1, sc2tog*, repeat until only a small stuffing hole remains.

BREAST PATCH, BEIGE

Wrap beige yarn once around finger and then work onto the resulting loop:

Rnd 1: Sc 10. Work round in a spiral, moving directly to the next row.

Rnd 2: 2 sc in each st = 20 sc.

Rnd 3: Sc 20.

Rnd 4: *Sc 1, 2 sc in next st*, repeat 10 times = 30 sc.

Rnd 5: Sc 30.

Rnd 6: *Sc 1, 2 sc in next st*, repeat 15 times = 45 sc.

Rnd 7: Sc 45.

BEAK, YELLOW

Ch 20 with yellow yarn, sl st to join in circle.

Rnd 1-2: Sc 20.

Rnd 3 to end: *Sc 1, sc2tog*, repeat until hole closes.

CREST, RED, 2 PCS

Wrap red yarn once around finger and then work onto the resulting loop:

Rnd 1: Sc 15. Work round in a spiral, moving directly to the next row.

Rnd 2: Sc 15.

Rnd 3: *Sc 1, sc2tog*, repeat 5 times = 10 sc.

Rnd 4-6: Sc 10.

Rnd 7: Sc2tog 5 = 5 sc.

FINISHING

Fill bird body piece with stuffing and sew filling hole closed. Sew breast patch onto body with matching thread. Sew beak onto body. Before making the final stitches, stuff beak. Sew a beige line across the middle of the beak. Sew crests onto top of body. Cut eyes out of white and black felt. Also cut eyebrows and tail out of black felt, and cheek patches out of burgundy. Glue or sew felt parts in place.

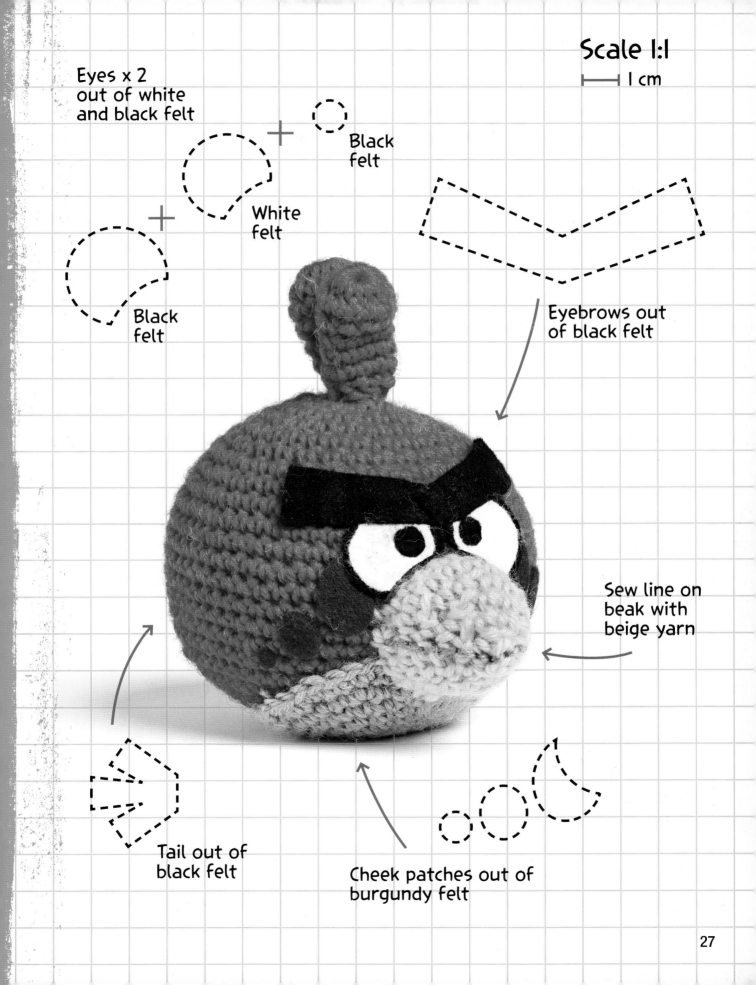

Eyes x 2
out of white
and black felt

Black
felt

White
felt

Black
felt

Eyebrows out
of black felt

Sew line on
beak with
beige yarn

Tail out of
black felt

Cheek patches out of
burgundy felt

BOMB

Watch out, pigs—Bomb has a short fuse. If Bomb notices anyone touching the birds' precious eggs, things tend to get hot. Bomb hisses and sputters, turning redder and redder until he finally explodes. Bomb loves blowing things up, but he isn't completely in control of his powers.

- Yarn: lightweight smooth black, gray, yellow, and beige
- Crochet hook
- Felt: white, black, gray, and red
- Stuffing

BODY, BLACK – CROCHETED FROM BOTTOM TO TOP

Wrap black yarn once around finger and then work onto the resulting loop:

Rnd 1: Sc 10. Work round in a spiral, moving directly to the next row.

Rnd 2: 2 sc in each st = 20 sc.

Rnd 3: Sc 20.

Rnd 4: *Sc 1, 2 sc in next st*, repeat 10 times = 30 sc.

Rnd 5-6: Sc 30.

Rnd 7: *Sc 1, 2 sc in next st*, repeat 15 times = 45 sc.

Rnd 8: Sc 45.

Rnd 9: *Sc 2, 2 sc in next st*, repeat 15 times = 60 sc.

Rnd 10: Sc 60.

Rnd 11: *Sc 5, 2 sc in next st*, repeat 10 times = 70 sc.

Rnd 12-26: Sc 70.

Rnd 27-30: *Sc 1, sc2tog*, repeat over 4 rounds, leaving a hole.

BEAK, YELLOW

Ch 25 with yellow yarn, sl st to join in circle.

Rnd 1–3: Sc 25.
Rnd 4: Sc2tog 2, sc 17, sc2tog 2 = 21 sc.
Rnd 5: Sc 21.
Rnd 6: Sc2tog 2, sc 13, sc2tog 2 = 17 sc.
Rnd 7: Sc 17.
Rnd 8 to end: *Sc2tog*, repeat until hole closes.

CREST, YELLOW AND BLACK

Wrap yellow yarn once around finger and then work onto the resulting loop:

Rnd 1: Sc 10. Work round in a spiral, moving directly to the next row.
Rnd 2: *Sc 1, 2 sc in next st*, repeat 5 times = 15 sc.
Rnd 3: Sc 15. Switch to black yarn.
Rnd 4: *Sc 1, sc2tog*, repeat 5 times = 10 sc.
Rnd 5–6: Sc 10.
Rnd 7: *Sc 3, sc2tog*, repeat twice = 8 sc.
Rnd 8–9: Sc 8.

BREAST PATCH, GRAY

Wrap gray yarn once around finger and then work onto the resulting loop:

Rnd 1: Sc 10. Work round in a spiral, moving directly to the next row.
Rnd 2: 2 sc in each st = 20 sc.
Rnd 3: Sc 20.
Rnd 4: *Sc 1, 2 sc in next st*, repeat 10 times = 30 sc.
Rnd 5: Sc 30.
Rnd 6: *Sc 1, 2 sc in next st*, repeat 15 times = 45 sc.
Rnd 7: Sc 45.
Rnd 8: *Sc 2, 2 sc in next st*, repeat 15 times = 60 sc.
Rnd 9: Sc 60.

FINISHING

Fill bird body piece with stuffing and sew filling hole closed. Sew breast patch onto body with matching yarn. Sew beak onto body. Before making the final stitches, stuff beak. Sew a beige line across the middle of the beak. Sew crest onto top of body. Cut eyes out of white, black, and gray felt. Also cut eyebrows out of red felt. Glue or sew felt parts in place.

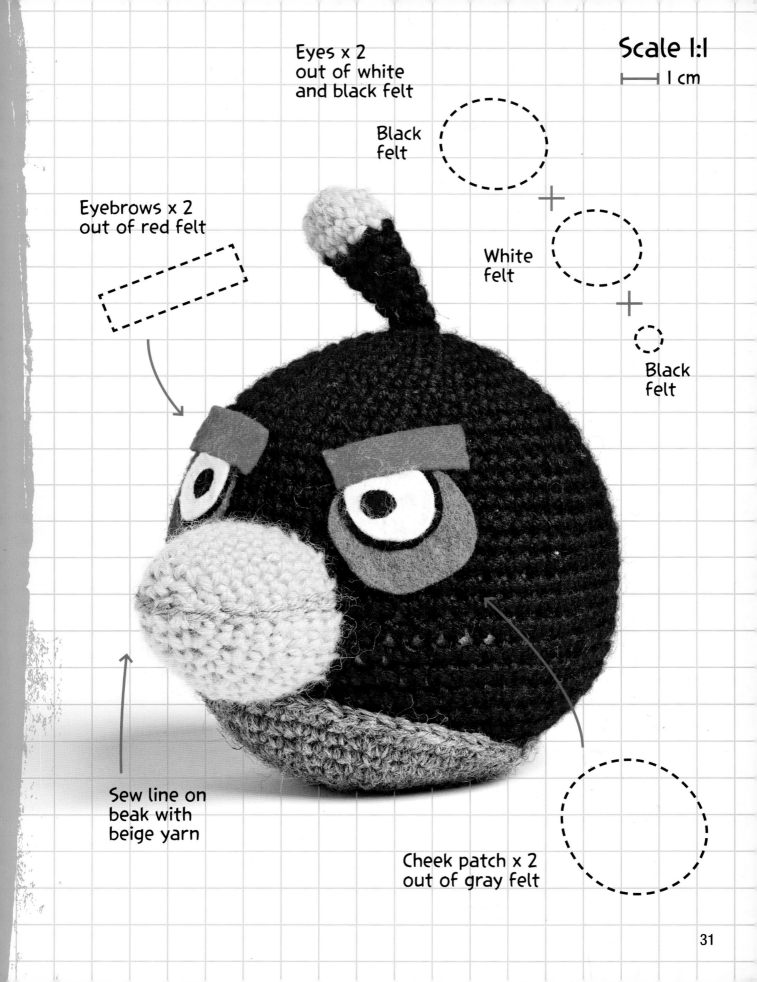

Eyes x 2
out of white
and black felt

Black
felt

Scale 1:1
├─┤ 1 cm

White
felt

Black
felt

Eyebrows x 2
out of red felt

Sew line on
beak with
beige yarn

Cheek patch x 2
out of gray felt

MATILDA

Matilda is the mother figure in the flock. She loves nature and tries to find peaceful solutions to conflict. But when she loses her temper, she really flies off the perch. Matilda's specialty is brewed herbal tea, which she uses to try to sooth Bomb's short fuse.

- Yarn: lightweight smooth white, beige, and yellow
- Crochet hook
- Felt: white, black, and yellow
- Stuffing

BODY, WHITE – CROCHETED FROM BOTTOM TO TOP

Wrap white yarn once around finger and then work onto the resulting loop:

Rnd 1: Sc 10. Work round in a spiral, moving directly to the next row.

Rnd 2: 2 sc in each st = 20 sc.

Rnd 3: Sc 20.

Rnd 4: *Sc 1, 2 sc in next st*, repeat 10 times = 30 sc.

Rnd 5: Sc 30.

Rnd 6: *Sc 1, 2 sc in next st*, repeat 15 times = 45 sc.

Rnd 7: 1 sc in each st = 45 sc.

Rnd 8: *Sc 2, 2 sc in next st*, repeat 15 times = 60 sc.

Rnd 9–12: Sc 60.

Rnd 13: *Sc 5, 2 sc in next st*, repeat 10 times = 70 sc.

Rnd 14–20: Sc 70.

Rnd 21: *Sc 5, sc2tog*, repeat 10 times = 60 sc.

Rnd 22–23: Sc 60.

Rnd 24: *Sc 4, sc2tog*, repeat 10 times = 50 sc.

Rnd 25–27: Sc 50.

Rnd 28: *Sc 3, sc2tog*, repeat 10 times = 40 sc.

Rnd 29: *Sc 3, sc2tog*, repeat 8 times = 32 sc.

Rnd 30: Sc 32.

Rnd 31: *Sc 2, sc2tog*, repeat 8 times = 24 sc.

Rnd 32: Sc 24.

Rnd 33 on: *Sc 1, sc2tog*, repeat until only a small stuffing hole remains.

BREAST PATCH, BEIGE

Wrap beige yarn once around finger and then work onto the resulting loop:

Rnd 1: Sc 10. Work round in a spiral, moving directly to the next row.

Rnd 2: 2 sc in each st = 20 sc.

Rnd 3: Sc 20.

Rnd 4: *Sc 1, 2 sc in next st*, repeat 10 times = 30 sc.

Rnd 5: Sc 30.

Rnd 6: *Sc 1, 2 sc in next st*, repeat 15 times = 45 sc.

Rnd 7: Sc 45.

Rnd 8: *Sc 2, 2 sc in next st*, repeat 15 times = 60 sc.

Rnd 9: Sc 60.

BEAK, YELLOW

Wrap yellow yarn once around finger and then work onto the resulting loop:

Rnd 1: Sc 7. Work round in a spiral, moving directly to the next row.

Rnd 2: Sc 3, *2 sc in next st* twice, sc 2 = 9 sc.

Rnd 3: Sc 3, *2 sc in next st*, repeat 3 times, sc 3 = 12 sc.

Rnd 4: Sc 3, *2 sc in next st*, repeat 6 times, sc 3 = 18 sc.

Rnd 5: Sc 18.

Rnd 6: Sc 7, *2 sc in next st*, repeat 4 times, sc 7 = 22 sc.

Rnd 7: Sc 22.

Rnd 8: Sc 7, *2 sc in next st*, repeat 8 times, sc 7 = 30 sc.

Rnd 9–10: Sc 30.

FINISHING

Fill bird body piece with stuffing and sew filling hole closed. Sew breast patch onto body with matching yarn. Sew beak onto body. Before making the final stitches, stuff beak. Sew a beige line across the middle of the beak. Cut eyes out of white and black felt. Also cut eyebrows, tail, and crest out of black felt, and cheek patches out of yellow. Glue or sew felt parts in place.

1 cm

Eyes x 2
out of
white and
black felt

Black felt

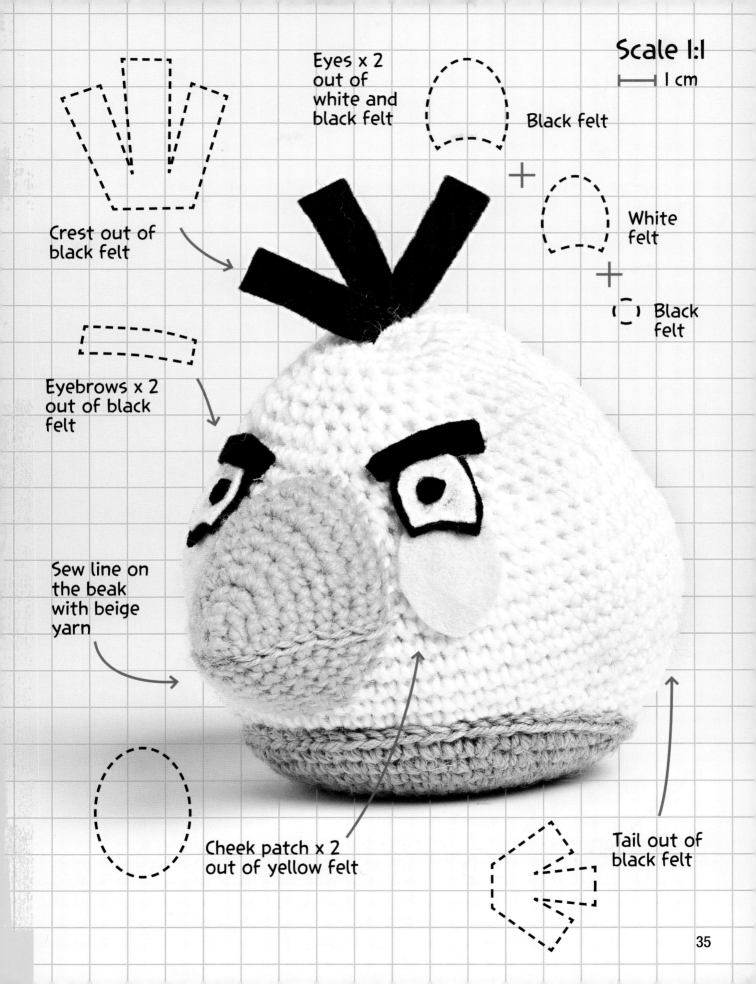

+

White
felt

+

Black
felt

Crest out of
black felt

Eyebrows x 2
out of black
felt

Sew line on
the beak
with beige
yarn

Cheek patch x 2
out of yellow felt

Tail out of
black felt

CHUCK

Chuck is the fastest of the birds. But although he has plenty of energy, he can't always seem to concentrate. Chuck acts before he thinks, which gets him into trouble.

- Yarn: lightweight smooth yellow, white, orange, and beige
- Crochet hook
- Felt: white, black, and red
- Stuffing

BODY, YELLOW – CROCHETED FROM BOTTOM TO TOP

Wrap yellow yarn once around finger and then work onto the resulting loop:

Rnd 1: Sc 10. Work round in a spiral, moving directly to the next row.

Rnd 2: 2 sc in each st = 20 sc.

Rnd 3: Sc 20.

Rnd 4: *Sc 1, 2 sc in next st*, repeat 10 times = 30 sc.

Rnd 5: Sc 30.

Rnd 6: *Sc 1, 2 sc in next st*, repeat 15 times = 45 sc.

Rnd 7: Sc 45.

Rnd 8: *Sc 2, 2 sc in next st*, repeat 15 times = 60 sc.

Rnd 9-10: Sc 60.

→

Rnd 11: *Sc 1, sc2tog*, repeat 20 times = 40 sc.
Rnd 12: Sc 40.
Rnd 13: *Sc 8, sc2tog*, repeat 4 times = 36 sc.
Rnd 14: Sc 36.
Rnd 15: *Sc 7, sc2tog*, repeat 4 times = 32 sc.
Rnd 16: Sc 32.
Rnd 17: *Sc 6, sc2tog*, repeat 4 times = 28 sc.
Rnd 18: Sc 28.
Rnd 19: *Sc 5, sc2tog*, repeat 4 times = 24 sc.
Rnd 20: Sc 24.
Rnd 21: *Sc 4, sc2tog*, repeat 4 times = 20 sc.
Rnd 22: Sc 20.
Rnd 23: *Sc 3, sc2tog*, repeat 4 times = 16 sc.
Rnd 24: Sc 16.
Rnd 25: *Sc 2, sc2tog*, repeat 4 times = 12 sc.
Rnd 26: *Sc2tog*, repeat until hole closes.

BREAST PATCH, WHITE

Wrap white yarn once around finger and then work onto the resulting loop:
Rnd 1: Sc 10. Work round in a spiral, moving directly to the next row.
Rnd 2: 2 sc in each st = 20 sc.
Rnd 3: Sc 20.
Rnd 4: *Sc 1, 2 sc in next st*, repeat 10 times = 30 sc.
Rnd 5: Sc 30.
Rnd 6: *Sc 1, 2 sc in next st*, repeat 15 times = 45 sc.

BEAK, ORANGE

Ch 15 with yellow yarn, sl st to join in circle.
Rnd 1-3: Sc 15.
Rnd 4 to end: *Sc 2, sc2tog*, repeat until hole closes.

FINISHING

Fill bird body piece with stuffing and sew filling hole closed. Sew breast patch onto body with matching yarn. Sew beak onto body. Before making the final stitches, stuff beak. Sew a beige line across the middle of the beak. Cut eyes out of white and black felt. Also cut a tail and crest out of black felt and eyebrows out of red. Glue or sew felt parts in place.

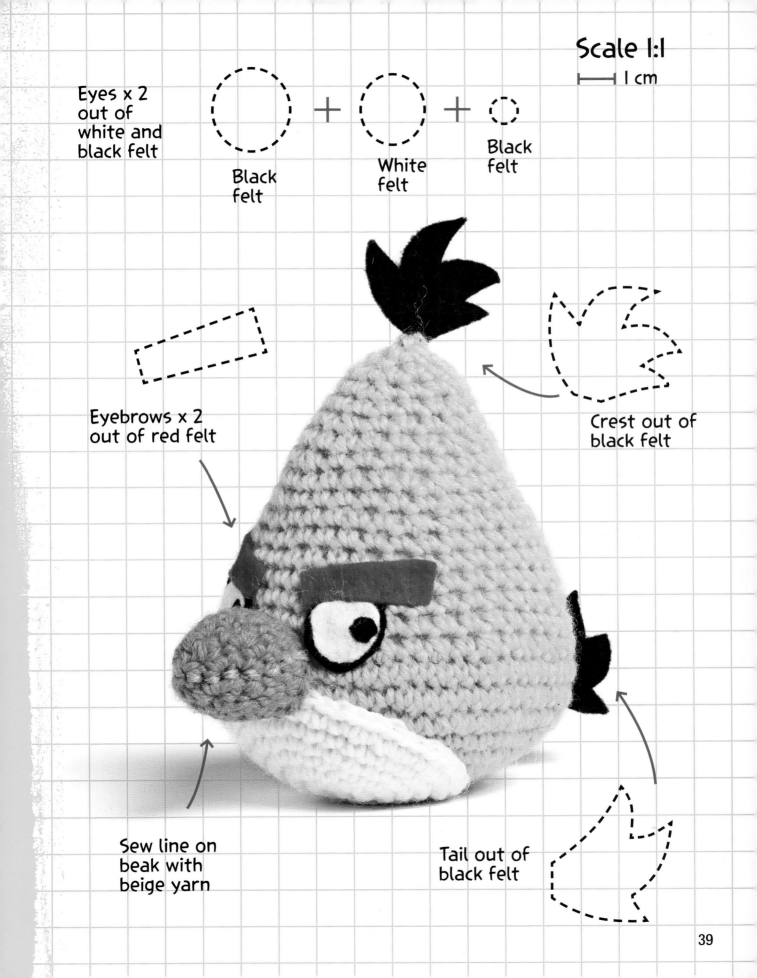

Eyes x 2 out of white and black felt

Black felt

+

White felt

+

Black felt

Scale 1:1

1 cm

Eyebrows x 2 out of red felt

Crest out of black felt

Sew line on beak with beige yarn

Tail out of black felt

JIM AND JAKE AND JAY

The Blues, Jim and Jake and Jay, are the youngest chicks in the flock. Hatched from the same egg, these brothers are little rascals with a habit for getting into trouble, because they like playing pranks. Even though such small birds might seem harmless, they are very energetic and clever.

- Yarn: lightweight smooth blue, yellow, and beige
- Crochet hook
- Felt: white, black, and red
- Stuffing

BODY, BLUE – CROCHETED FROM TOP TO BOTTOM

Wrap blue yarn once around finger and then work onto the resulting loop:

Rnd 1: Sc 10. Work round in a spiral, moving directly to the next row.

Rnd 2: 2 sc in each st = 20 sc.

Rnd 3: Sc 20.

Rnd 4: *Sc 1, 2 sc in next st*, repeat 10 times = 30 sc.

Rnd 5: Sc 30.

Rnd 6: *Sc 1, 2 sc in next st*, repeat 15 times = 45 sc.

Rnd 7-16: Sc 45.

→

Rnd 17: *Sc 1, sc2tog*, repeat 15 times = 30 sc.

Rnd 18: Sc 30.

Rnd 19: *Sc 1, sc2tog*, repeat 10 times = 20 sc.

Rnd 20: Sc 20.

Rnd 21 on: *Sc 1, sc2tog*, repeat until only a small stuffing hole remains.

BEAK, YELLOW

Ch 15 with yellow yarn, sl st to join in circle.

Rnd 1-3: Sc 15.

Rnd 4 to end: *Sc 1, sc2tog*, repeat until hole closes.

CREST, BLUE, 2 PCS

Wrap blue yarn once around finger and then work onto the resulting loop:

Rnd 1: Sc 10. Work round in a spiral, moving directly to the next row.

Rnd 2-5: Sc 10.

Rnd 6: *Sc2tog*, repeat 5 times = 5 sc.

FINISHING

Fill bird body piece with stuffing and sew filling hole closed. Sew beak onto body. Before making the final stitches, stuff beak. Sew a beige line across the middle of the beak. Sew crests onto top of body, one in front of the other. Cut eyes out of white, black, and red felt. Also cut tail out of black felt. Glue or sew felt parts in place.

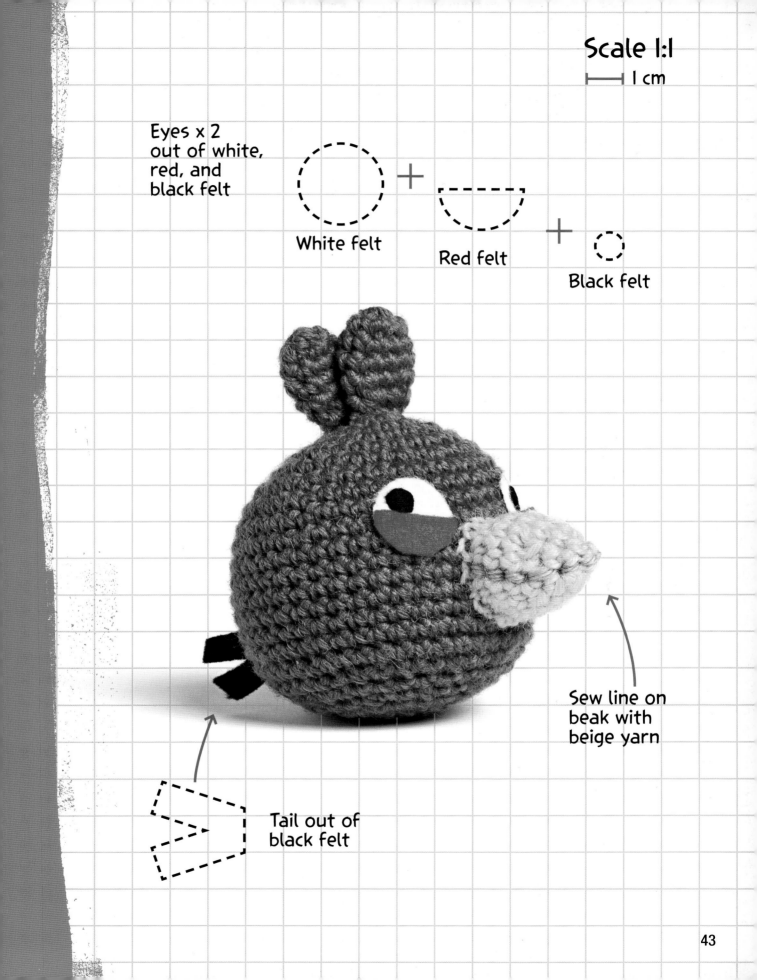

Scale 1:1

⊢——⊣ 1 cm

Eyes x 2
out of white,
red, and
black felt

White felt   +   Red felt   +   Black felt

Sew line on
beak with
beige yarn

Tail out of
black felt

THE EGGS

The eggs are the white apples of the Angry Birds' eyes. Red holds tight to the belief that one day they will hatch. The birds guard the eggs with their lives, but every once in a while the pigs surprise them and succeed in carrying off the eggs.

- Yarn: lightweight smooth white
- Crochet hook
- Stuffing

BODY, WHITE – CROCHETED FROM BOTTOM TO TOP

Wrap white yarn once around finger and then work onto the resulting loop:

Rnd 1: Sc 10. Work round in a spiral, moving directly to the next row.

Rnd 2: 2 sc in each st = 20 sc.

Rnd 3: Sc 20.

Rnd 4: *Sc 1, 2 sc in next st*, repeat 10 times = 30 sc.

Rnd 5: Sc 30.

Rnd 6: *Sc 1, 2 sc in next st*, repeat 15 times = 45 sc.

Rnd 7-9: Sc 45.

Rnd 10: *Sc 4, 2 sc in next st*, repeat 9 times = 54 sc.

Rnd 11-16: Sc 54.

Rnd 17: *Sc 4, sc2tog*, repeat 9 times = 45 sc.

Rnd 18-22: Sc 45.

Rnd 23: *Sc 3, sc2tog*, repeat 9 times = 36 sc.

Rnd 24: Sc 36.

Rnd 25-30: *Sc 3, sc2tog*, repeat for 7 rows until only a small stuffing hole remains.

FINISHING

Fill piece with stuffing and sew filling hole closed.

KING PIG

King Pig is the absolute ruler of Piggy Island. He is always hungry, so his subjects have to work frantically to keep him fed. The king's favorite food is eggs, even though he hasn't ever tasted them. His big secret is that there actually isn't a single egg in his treasury.

- Yarn: lightweight smooth green and yellow
- Crochet hook
- Felt: white, black, light and dark green
- Blue beads
- Stuffing

BODY, GREEN – CROCHETED FROM BOTTOM TO TOP

Wrap green yarn once around finger and then work onto the resulting loop:

Rnd 1: Sc 10. Work round in a spiral, moving directly to the next row.

Rnd 2: 2 sc in each st = 20 sc.

Rnd 3: Sc 20.

Rnd 4: *Sc 1, 2 sc in next st*, repeat 10 times = 30 sc.

→

Rnd 5–6: Sc 30.

Rnd 7: *Sc 1, 2 sc in next st*, repeat 15 times = 45 sc.

Rnd 8: Sc 45.

Rnd 9: *Sc 2, 2 sc in next st*, repeat 15 times = 60 sc.

Rnd 10: Sc 60.

Rnd 11: *Sc 2, 2 sc in next st*, repeat 20 times = 80 sc.

Rnd 12: Sc 80.

Rnd 13: *Sc 3, 2 sc in next st*, repeat 20 times = 100 sc.

Rnd 14–15: Sc 100.

Rnd 16: *Sc 3, 2 sc in next st*, repeat 25 times = 125 sc.

Rnd 17–24: Sc 125.

Rnd 25: *Sc 3, sc2tog*, repeat 25 times = 100 sc.

Rnd 26–38: Sc 100.

Rnd 39: *Sc 3, sc2tog*, repeat 20 times = 80 sc.

Rnd 40–48: Sc 80.

Rnd 49: *Sc 2, sc2tog*, repeat 20 times = 60 sc.

Rnd 50: Sc 60.

Rnd 51: *Sc 2, sc2tog*, repeat 15 times = 45 sc.

Rnd 52: Sc 45.

Rnd 53 on: *Sc 1, sc2tog*, repeat until only a small stuffing hole remains.

NOSE, GREEN

Wrap green yarn once around finger and then work onto the resulting loop:

Rnd 1: Sc 10. Work round in a spiral, moving directly to the next row.

Rnd 2: *2 sc in next st*, repeat 10 times = 20 sc.

Rnd 3: Sc 20.

Rnd 4: *Sc 1, 2 sc in next st*, repeat 10 times = 30 sc.

Rnd 5: Sc 30.

Rnd 6: *Sc 1, 2 sc in next st*, repeat 15 times = 45 sc.

Rnd 7: Sc 45.

Now work flat for a little while.

Turn piece. Work 1 ch and 10 sc.

Turn piece. Work 1 ch, sc 10, sc 1 between the rows crocheted before and sc 22 along the side of the snout.

Turn piece. Work 1 ch and sc 10.

Turn piece. Work 1 ch, sc 10, sc 1 between the rows crocheted before, sc 13 along the edge of the snout, sc 1 between the rows crocheted before, and sc 10.

Sc around snout 5 times.

EARS, GREEN, 2 PCS

Wrap green yarn once around finger and then work onto the resulting loop:

Rnd 1: Sc 10. Work round in a spiral, moving directly to the next row.
Rnd 2: 2 sc in each st = 20 sc.
Rnd 3: Sc 20.
Rnd 4: Sc 10.

CROWN, YELLOW

Ch 25, sl st to join in circle.
Rnd 1–8: Sc 25.

Five points are worked onto the crown. Work each point, which is 5 stitches wide, as follows:

Rnd 1–3: Sc 5. Continue back and forth, i.e. turning at the end of each row, and then work 1 sl st at the beginning of the row (= turning chain).
Rnd 4: Turn piece and ch 1. Sc2tog and sc 3 = 4 sc.
Rnd 5: Turn piece and ch 1. Sc2tog and sc 2 = 3 sc.
Rnd 6: Turn piece and ch 1. Sc2tog and sc 1 = 2 sc.
Rnd 7: Turn piece and ch 1. Crochet 2 remaining sts together = 1 sc. Do not cut yarn.
Using sl st, move down along left edge of point. Work next crown point as previous.
Once you have crocheted all five points, work the pointed edge of the crown with scs.

FINISHING

Fill body piece with stuffing and sew filling hole closed. Sew snout onto body. Stuff it before making final stitches. Sew ears in place. Cut eyes out of white, black, and light green felt. Also cut mouth and nostrils out of black felt, and eyebrows and insides of ears out of green. Glue or sew felt parts in place. Sew blue beads onto crown and attach crown to head.

Inside of ear x 2
out of green felt

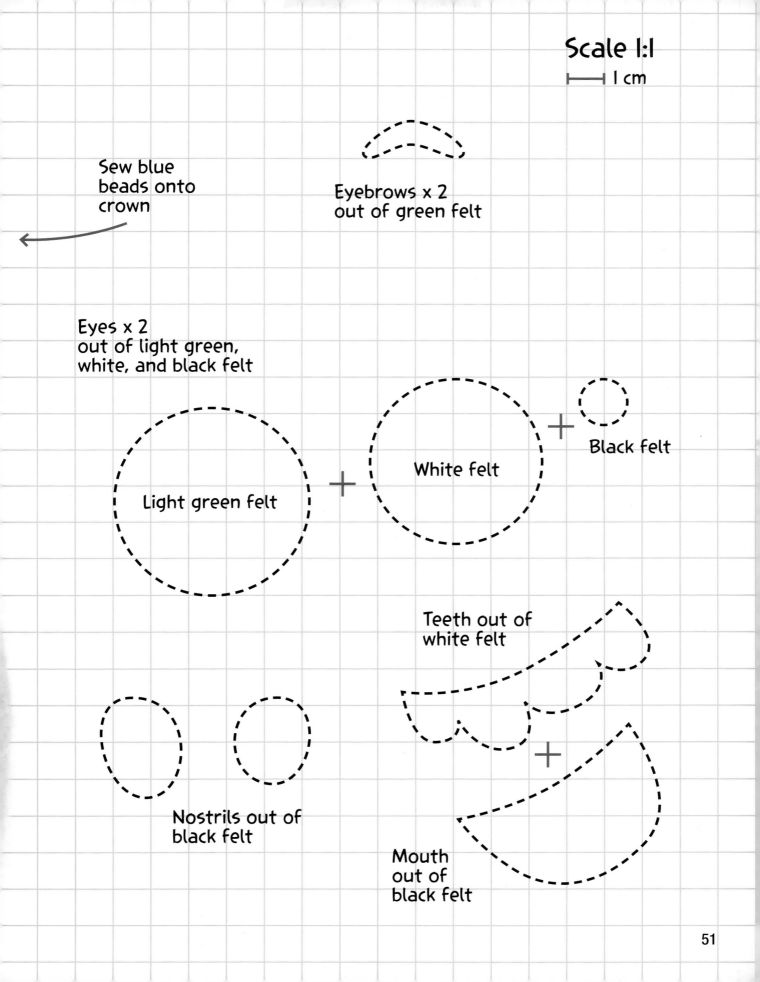

Scale 1:1

├──┤ 1 cm

Sew blue
beads onto
crown

Eyebrows x 2
out of green felt

Eyes x 2
out of light green,
white, and black felt

White felt

Black felt

Light green felt

+

+

Teeth out of
white felt

+

Nostrils out of
black felt

Mouth
out of
black felt

CORPORAL PIG

Corporal Pig is the loyal chief of the king's army.
He leads his troops tirelessly from defeat to defeat.

- Yarn: lightweight smooth green, gray, brown, and black
- Crochet hook
- Felt: white, black, pink, and burgundy
- Stuffing

BODY, GREEN – CROCHETED FROM BOTTOM TO TOP

Wrap green yarn once around finger and then work onto the resulting loop:

Rnd 1: Sc 10. Work round in a spiral, moving directly to the next row.

Rnd 2: 2 sc in each st = 20 sc.

Rnd 3: Sc 20.

Rnd 4: *Sc 1, 2 sc in next st*, repeat 10 times = 30 sc.

Rnd 5: Sc 30.

Rnd 6: *Sc 1, 2 sc in next st*, repeat 15 times = 45 sc.

Rnd 7: Sc 45.

Rnd 8: *Sc 2, 2 sc in next st*, repeat 15 times = 60 sc.

Rnd 9-11: Sc 60.

Rnd 12: *Sc 2, 2 sc in next st*, repeat 20 times = 80 sc.

Rnd 13-26: Sc 80.

→

Rnd 27: *Sc 2, sc2tog*, repeat 20 times = 60 sc.

Rnd 28: Sc 60.

Rnd 29: *Sc 2, sc2tog*, repeat 15 times = 45 sc.

Rnd 30: Sc 45.

Rnd 31: *Sc 1, sc2tog*, repeat 15 times = 30 sc.

Rnd 32: Sc 30.

Rnd 33 on: *Sc 1, sc2tog*, repeat until only a small stuffing hole remains.

NOSE, GREEN

Wrap green yarn once around finger and then work onto the resulting loop:

Rnd 1: Sc 10. Work round in a spiral, moving directly to the next row.

Rnd 2: 2 sc in each st = 20 sc.

Rnd 3: Sc 20.

Rnd 4: *2 sc in next st*, repeat 15 times, sc 5 = 35 sc.

Rnd 5: *Sc 5, Sc2tog*, repeat 5 times = 30 sc.

Rnd 6-8: Sc 30.

HELMET, GRAY

Wrap gray yarn once around finger and then work onto the resulting loop:

Rnd 1: Sc 10. Work round in a spiral, moving directly to the next row.

Rnd 2: 2 sc in each st = 20 sc.

Rnd 3: Sc 20.

Rnd 4: *Sc 1, 2 sc in next st*, repeat 10 times = 30 sc.

Rnd 5: Sc 30.

Rnd 6: *Sc 1, 2 sc in next st*, repeat 15 times = 45 sc.

Rnd 7: Sc 45.

Rnd 8: *Sc 2, 2 sc in next st*, repeat 15 times = 60 sc.

Rnd 9: Sc 60.

Rnd 10: *Sc 2, 2 sc in next st*, repeat 20 times = 80 sc.

Rnd 11-24: Sc 80.

Rnd 25: *Sc 8, sc2tog*, repeat 8 times = 72 sc.

Rnd 26: Sc 72.

HELMET STRAPS, BROWN, 2 PCS

Crochet 5 chain stitches (ch) for starting chain.

Rnd 1-11: Sc 4 (always turn piece at the end of the row and ch 1 as turning chain).

FINISHING

Fill body piece with stuffing and sew filling hole closed. Sew snout onto body. Stuff it before making final stitches. Sew straps to helmet and place helmet on pigs head. You can sew dents in the helmet with black yarn. Cut eyes out of white, black, and pink felt. Also cut mouth and nostrils out of black felt, teeth out of white, and tongue parts out of pink and burgundy. Glue or sew felt parts in place.

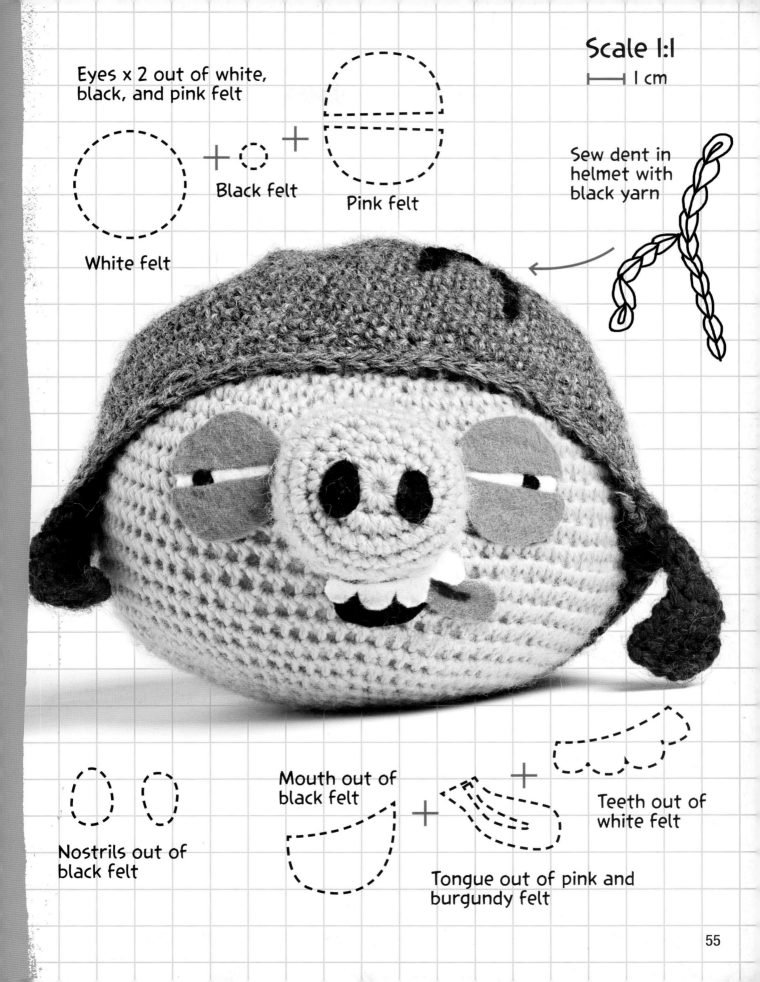

Eyes x 2 out of white, black, and pink felt

Black felt

Pink felt

White felt

Scale 1:1

⊢—⊣ 1 cm

Sew dent in helmet with black yarn

Nostrils out of black felt

Mouth out of black felt

Tongue out of pink and burgundy felt

Teeth out of white felt

MINION PIG

The Minion Pigs do their best to find eggs for their king. They are the lowest of the low in piggy society, but they are still happy with their lives.

- Yarn: lightweight smooth green
- Crochet hook
- Felt: white, black, and green
- Stuffing

BODY, GREEN – CROCHETED FROM TOP TO BOTTOM.

Wrap green yarn once around finger and then work onto the resulting loop:

Rnd 1: Sc 10. Work round in a spiral, moving directly to the next row.

Rnd 2: 2 sc in each st = 20 sc.

Rnd 3: Sc 20.

Rnd 4: *Sc 1, 2 sc in next st*, repeat 10 times = 30 sc.

Rnd 5: Sc 30.

Rnd 6: *Sc 1, 2 sc in next st*, repeat 15 times = 45 sc.

Rnd 7: 1 sc in each st = 45 sc.

Rnd 8: *Sc 2, 2 sc in next st*, repeat 15 times = 60 sc.

Rnd 9-16: Sc 60.

Rnd 17: *Sc 2, sc2tog*, repeat 15 times = 45 sc.

Rnd 18: Sc 45.

Rnd 19: *Sc 1, sc2tog*, repeat 15 times = 30 sc.

Rnd 20: Sc 30.

Rnd 21 on: *Sc 1, sc2tog*, repeat until only a small stuffing hole remains.

NOSE, GREEN

Wrap green yarn once around finger and then work onto the resulting loop:

Rnd 1: Sc 10. Work round in a spiral, moving directly to the next row.

Rnd 2: *2 sc in each st*, repeat 6 times, sc 4 = 16 sc.

Rnd 3: Sc 16.

Rnd 4: 2 sc in each st = 32 sc.

Rnd 5: Sc 32.

Rnd 6: Sc2tog 16 = 16 sc.

EARS, GREEN, 2 PCS

Wrap green yarn once around finger and then work onto the resulting loop:

Rnd 1: Sc 10. Work round in a spiral, moving directly to the next row.

Rnd 2: Sc 10.

FINISHING

Fill body piece with stuffing and sew filling hole closed. Sew snout onto body. Stuff it before making final stitches. Sew ears in place. Cut eyes out of white and black felt. Also cut mouth and nostrils out of black felt, teeth out of white, and eyebrows and insides of ears out of green. Glue or sew felt parts in place.

⊢━━━┥ 1 cm

Eyes x 2 out of
white and black felt

White felt ✛ Black felt

Inside of ear x 2
out of green felt

Eyebrows x 2
out of green felt

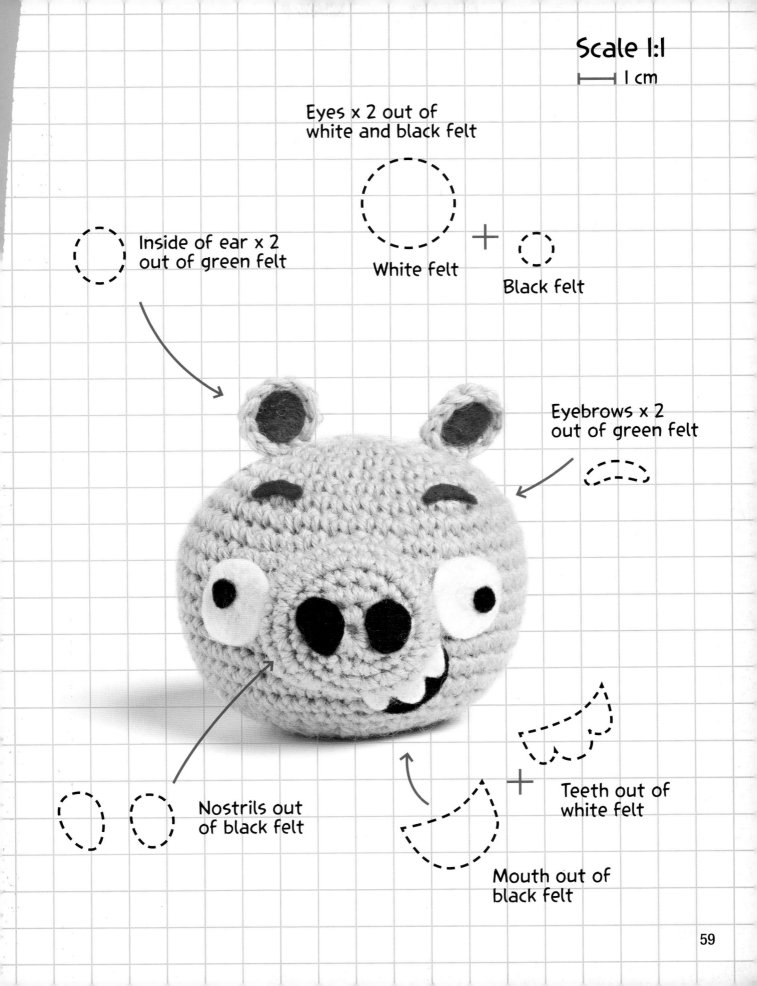

Nostrils out
of black felt

Teeth out of
white felt

✛

Mouth out of
black felt

WOOD, STONE, AND ICE BLOCKS

The pigs' teetering towers are made out of wood, stone, and ice.

- Yarn: lightweight smooth light brown / brown (wood), light gray / gray (stone), and light blue / white (ice)
- Crochet hook
- Stuffing

LARGE BLOCK, FRAME

Crochet 21 chain stitches (ch) for starting chain.

Rnd 1-25: Sc 20 (always turn piece at the end of the row and ch 1 as turning chain).

LARGE BLOCK, BLOCK ENDS, 2 PCS

Crochet 9 chain stitches (ch) for starting chain.

Rnd 1-6: Sc 8 (always turn piece at the end of the row and ch 1 as turning chain).

SMALL BLOCK, FRAME

Crochet 16 chain stitches (ch) for starting chain.

Rnd 1-20: Sc 15 (always turn piece at the end of the row and ch 1 as turning chain).

SMALL BLOCK, BLOCK ENDS, 2 PCS

Crochet 7 chain stitches (ch) for starting chain.

Rnd 1-4: Sc 6 (always turn piece at the end of the row and ch 1 as turning chain).

BLOCK FINISHING

Sew rectangle on the wider side to make a cylinder. Sew each end piece onto an end of the cylinder. Now the cylinder should begin looking like a block. Before making the final stitches, stuff the block. Work a single crochet border along the sides of the block to make it stand up better. See picture.

SLINGSHOT

The frame of the slingshot is cut out of plywood, which is then covered with a crocheted surface. This works as a launch pad for your birds' flights.

- Yarn: lightweight smooth light brown
- Crochet hook
- Plywood
- Jigsaw
- Leather
- Rubber band

MAKING SLINGSHOT OUT OF WOOD

Cut a piece of plywood according to the shape provided on the next two pages (pp. 64–65).

The slingshot in the picture has been covered with a crocheted surface. Assuming you cut the plywood using the dimensions provided, crochet the surface as follows:

SLINGSHOT CURVE, LIGHT BROWN, 2 PCS

Wrap light brown yarn once around finger and then work onto the resulting loop:

Rnd I: Sc 15. Work round in a spiral, moving directly to the next row.

Rnd 2–33: Sc 15.

After this, work flat (not in the round).

Rnd 34–36: Sc 9 (turn piece at the end of each row, ch 1 at the beginning of each row).

SLINGSHOT HANDLE, LIGHT BROWN

Wrap light brown yarn once around finger and then work onto the resulting loop:

Rnd I: Sc 15. Work round in a spiral, moving directly to the next row.

Rnd 2–27: Sc 15.

Sew the crocheted covers together over the wood slingshot.

Attach elastic bands with piece of leather to slingshot fork.

Scale 1:1

├── 1 cm

Combine patterns and cut
a piece of plywood in the
shape of the pattern.

Attach rubber bands
to a piece of leather
this size.

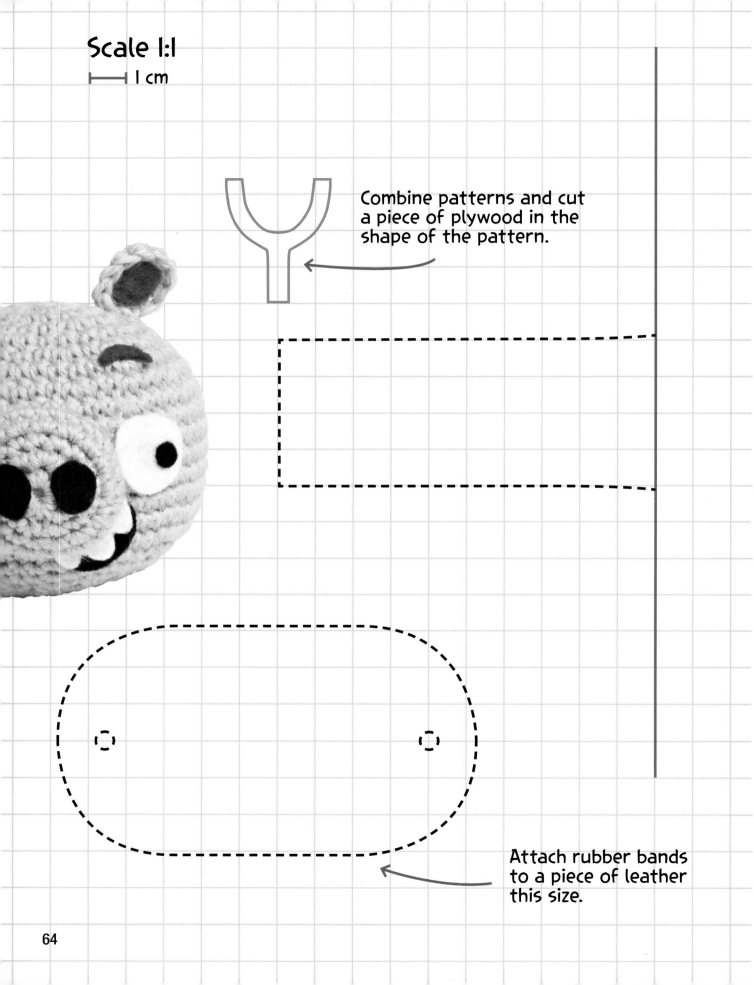

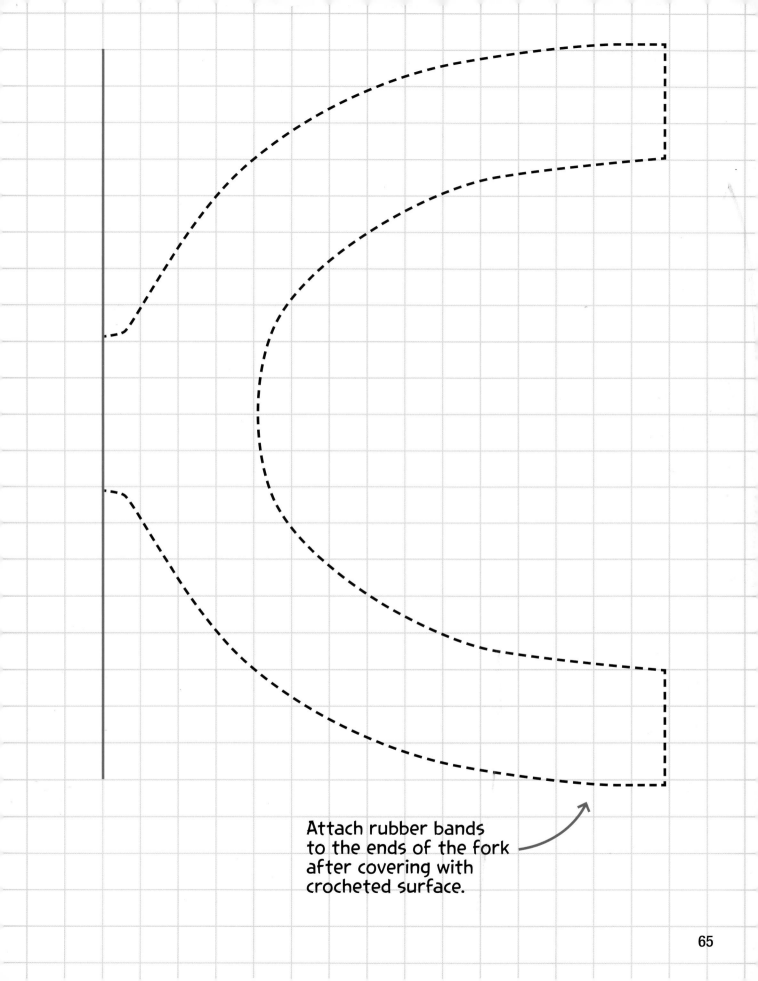

Attach rubber bands to the ends of the fork after covering with crocheted surface.

LET THE GAMES BEGIN!

CROCHET YOURSELF SOME BIRD-WEAR!

Now you've mastered the art of Amigurumi, it's time to take your needlework to the next level! The next chapter uses many of the same crocheting techniques to produce some great knitwear for you and any young Angry Birds in the making. These pieces are a little more challenging so don't get disheartened if they take a bit longer to master. Just think how bird-tastic you'll turn out looking in the end!

SILLY SNOUT HAT

SIZE Circumference 48 cm.
YARN Lightweight smooth green, white, and gray.
CROCHET HOOK Size needed to obtain gauge.
OTHER MATERIALS Two small black button eyes and stuffing for snout.
STITCH PATTERNS Crochet sc according to pattern.
GAUGE 18 single crochet = 10 cm.

HAT

Wrap green yarn once around finger and crochet in spiral, moving directly to the next row.

Rnd 1: Sc 8.

Rnd 2: 2 sc in each st = 16 sc.

Rnd 3: *Sc 1, 2 sc in next st*, repeat 8 times = 24 sc.

Rnd 4: *Sc 2, 2 sc in next st*, repeat 8 times = 32 sc.

Rnd 5: 1 sc in each st = 32 sc.

Rnd 6: *Sc 3, 2 sc in next st*, repeat 8 times = 40 sc.

Rnd 7: 1 sc in each st = 40 sc. Continue increasing in this way every 2nd row until work is 80 sc. Each increasing round adds 8 sc. When the work is 80 sc, stop increasing and sc 5 rnds without increasing.

→

Begin crocheting eyes. First make a small ball of white yarn for each eye.

Rnd 1: In white, 2 sc in each of next three sts = 6 sc. Set white yarn aside behind work and 19 sc in green. Take up white yarn and 2 sc in each of next three sts = 6 sc. Set white yarn aside behind work. Take up green and work 1 sc in each st around until you reach the first eye.

Rnd 2: Take up white yarn and 2 sc in first white st, 4 sc and then 2 sc in next st = 8 sc. Switch yarn and 18 sc in green. Switch yarn and work second eye as first. Set white yarn aside behind work and work around hat in green.

Rnd 3: Take up white yarn and 2 sc in first white st, 6 sc and then 2 sc in next st = 10 sc. Switch yarn and 18 sc in green. Work second eye as first. Set white yarn aside behind work and work around hat in green.

Rnd 4–6: Take up white yarn and 10 sc. Switch yarn and 18 sc in green. Work second eye as first. Set white yarn aside behind work and work around hat in green.

Rnd 7: Take up white yarn and 1 sc in first st, skip 1 st, 1 sc in next st, 5 sc, skip 1 st, and 1 sc in next st = 8 sc. Switch yarn and 18 sc in green. Work second eye as first. Set white yarn aside behind work and work around hat in green.

Rnd 8: Take up white yarn and 1 sc in first st, skip 1 st, 4 sc, skip 1 st, and 1 sc in next st = 6 sc. Switch yarn and 18 sc in green. Work second eye as first. Set white yarn aside behind work and work around hat in green.

Rnd 9: Take up white yarn and 1 sc in first white st, *skip 1 st and 1 sc in next st*, repeat 3 times = 4 sc. Switch yarn and 18 sc in green. Work second eye as first. Work around hat in green. Continue working in green. At eyes work twice sc2tog (i.e. decrease 2 sts). Continue with 1 sc in each st until you have worked 2.5 cm in green above the eyes.

→

EAR FLAPS (2 PCS)

Wrap green yarn once around finger and crochet in spiral, moving directly to the next row.

Rnd 1: Sc 8.

Rnd 2: 2 sc in each st = 16 sc.

Rnd 3: *Sc 1, 2 sc in next st*, repeat 8 times = 24 sc.

Rnd 4: *Sc 2, 2 sc in next st*, repeat 8 times = 32 sc.

Rnd 5: 1 sc in each st = 32 sc.

Rnd 6: *Sc 2, 2 sc in next st*, repeat 8 times, sc 5 = 41 sc.

Attach ear flaps to sides of hat, inside, so that more than half of the flaps extend below the edge of the hat. Work 2 rnds sc around the edges of hat and flaps. On the last round, work "tails" at the tips of each flap. Work the round until you are at the middle of the first flap, then 17 ch, 1 sc in 2nd ch from hook, and 1 sc in each ch. Continue working around and do the same thing when you reach the second flap. Close round with slip st and fasten off.

SNOUT

Chain 6 in green as starting chain.

Rnd 1: Sc in 2nd ch from hook, sc 1 in each starting chain st = 5 sts.

Rnd 2: Ch 1, 2 sc in first st, sc 3 and sc 2 in last st = 7 sts.

Rnd 3: Ch 1, 2 sc in first st, sc 5 and sc 2 in last st = 9 sts.

Rnd 4: Ch 1, 2 sc in first st, sc 7 and sc 2 in last st = 11 sts.

Rnd 5: Ch 1, 2 sc in first st, sc 9 and sc 2 in last st = 13 sc.

Rnd 10–11: Ch 1 and 1 sc in each st = 13 sc.

Rnd 12: Ch 1, skip one st and sc 12 = 12 sc.

Rnd 13: Ch 1, skip one st and sc 11 = 11 sc.

Rnd 14: Ch 1, skip one st and sc 10 = 10 sc.

Rnd 15: Ch 1, skip one st and sc 9 = 9 sc.

Rnd 16–19: Sc around edge.

EARS (2 PCS)

Wrap green yarn once around finger and crochet in a spiral, sc 8. Continue working in a spiral, moving directly to the next row.

Rnd 1: 2 sc in each st = 16 sc.

Rnd 2: *Sc 1, 2 sc in next st*, repeat 8 times = 24 sc.

Rnd 3: *Sc 2, 2 sc in next st*, repeat 8 times = 32 sc.

Rnd 4: Sc 32. Crochet another similar piece.

FINISHING

Steam hat lightly. Finish pig face as pictured. Fill snout lightly with stuffing and sew to hat. Sew buttons to eyes. Sew on ears. Embroider nostrils to snout with gray yarn in satin stitch and cable stitch eyebrows above eyes.

RICOCHET CROCHET CAP

SIZE Circumference 54–48 cm.
YARN Lightweight smooth red, yellow, light brown, white, and black.
CROCHET HOOK Size needed to obtain gauge.
OTHER MATERIALS A little stuffing for beak.
STITCH PATTERNS Crochet sc according to pattern.
GAUGE 17 single crochet = 10 cm.
NOTES Cap crocheted from top of head down.

HEAD FEATHERS

Wrap red yarn once around finger and then work onto the resulting loop:

Rnd I: Sc 6. Work round in a spiral, moving directly to the next row.

Rnd 2: Sc 2 in each st = 12 sc.

Rnd 3: 1 sc in each st = 12 sc. Repeat rnd 3 until work height is 5 cm. Work next round *Sc 1, skip 1 st*, repeat 6 times = 6 sc. Fasten off. Work second feather the same way, do not break yarn, but remove hook from loop. Hold feathers together so piece with free loop is to the back. Insert hook from inside of forward feather through stitch of last row and into next loop from free loop of back feather and pull yarn through. Attach feathers to each other with three slip stitches. Do not break thread—continue crocheting hat.

→

STOCKING CAP

Rnd 1: Ch 1 and begin crocheting around both feathers. Sc 8 around one feather, ch 1 to move to second feather and sc 1 around that one as well = 18 sts.

Rnd 2: *Sc 1, 2 sc in next st*, repeat 9 times = 27 sc.

Rnd 3-4: 1 sc in each st = 27 sc.

Rnd 5: *2 sc in next st, 1 sc *, repeat 3 times, sc 2 in next st = 41 sc.

Rnd 6-7: 1 sc in each st = 41 sc.

Rnd 8: *Sc 2, 2 sc in next st*, repeat 13 times, sc 2 = 54 sc.

Rnd 9-11: 1 sc in each st = 54 sc.

Rnd 12: *Sc 2, 2 sc in next st*, repeat 18 times = 72 sc.

Rnd 13-15: 1 sc in each st = 72 sc.

Rnd 16: *Sc 2, 2 sc in next st*, repeat 24 times = 96 sc.

Rnd 17-29: 1 sc in each st = 96 sc.

Rnd 30: *Sc 31, skip one st*, repeat 3 times = 93 sc.

Mark front center point of hat and work in tapestry crochet from first round of chart. Arrow at lower edge of chart marks hat center point. Count starting point from here. Work rounds 1-4 of chart, decreasing 3 sc from red portion of each until hat is desired size. Finish with two rounds of all light brown yarn. Fasten off.

BEAK

Wrap yellow yarn once around finger and then work onto the resulting loop:

Rnd 1: Sc. Work in a spiral, moving directly to the next round.

Rnd 2: 1 sc in each st = 7 sc.

Rnd 3: *Sc 1, 2 sc in next st*, repeat 3 times, sc 1 = 10 sc.

Rnd 4: 1 sc in each st = 10 sc.

Rnd 5: *Sc 1, 2 sc in next st*, repeat 5 times = 15 sc.

Rnd 6-7: 1 sc in each st = 15 sc.

Rnd 8: *2 sc in next st, 1 sc in next st*, repeat 7 times, sc 1 = 22 sc.

Rnd 9-10: 1 sc in each st = 22 sc.

Rnd 11: slip st 1 in each st. Cut the thread and decorate beak with black yarn. Fill beak with stuffing and sew to upper part of light brown curve.

→

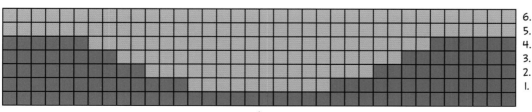

6.
5.
4.
3.
2.
1.

↑stocking cap center

EYES

Wrap white yarn once around finger and then work onto the resulting loop:

Rnd 1: Sc. Work in a spiral, moving directly to the next round.

Rnd 2: 2 sc in each st of previous rnd = 14 sc.

Rnd 3: *Sc 1, 2 sc in next st*, repeat 7 times = 21 sc.

Rnd 4: *Sc 1, 2 sc in next st*, repeat 10 times, sc 1 = 31 sc.

Rnd 5: slip st 1 in each st. Fasten off. Crochet another similar piece. Decorate eyes with black yarn. Sew eyes to stocking cap.

EYEBROWS

With black yarn, crochet 24 chain stitches (ch) for starting chain.

Rnd 1: Sc in 2nd ch from hook, sc 1 in each starting chain st = 23 sts.

Rnd 2: T-ch 1, 11 sc, skip 1 and 11 sc = 22 sc.

Rnd 3: T-ch 1, 10 sc, skip 2 and 10 sc = 20 sc. Sew eyebrows above eyes.

BLASTING CAP

SIZE Circumference approx. 56 cm.
YARN Lightweight smooth black, gray, yellow, red, and white.
CROCHET HOOK Size needed to obtain gauge.
STITCH PATTERNS Single crochet according to instructions.
GAUGE 18 single crochet = 10 cm.

STOCKING CAP

Wrap black yarn once around finger and then work 9 sc onto the resulting loop. Work round in a spiral, moving directly to the next row.

Rnd 2: Sc 2 in each st = 18 sc.

Rnd 3: *Sc 1, 2 sc in next st*, repeat 9 times = 27 sc.

Rnd 4: 1 sc in each st = 27 sc.

Rnd 5: *2 sc in next st, 1 sc *, repeat 13 times, sc 2 in next st = 41 sc.

Rnd 6-7: 1 sc in each st = 41 sc.

Rnd 8: *Sc 2, 2 sc in next st*, repeat 13 times, sc 2 = 54 sc.

Rnd 9-11: 1 sc in each st = 54 sc.

Rnd 12: *Sc 2, 2 sc in next st*, repeat 18 times = 72 sc.

Rnd 13-15: 1 sc in each st = 72 sc.

Rnd 16: *Sc 2, 2 sc in next st*, repeat 24 times = 96 sc.

Rnd 17-29: 1 sc in each st = 96 sc.

→

Continue without increasing until the hat is about 18 cm high. Change to gray yarn and sc until yarn runs out. During gray rounds, decrease 3 each round as necessary until stocking cap size is appropriate. Slip st one more round in white.

BEAK

Ch 11 in yellow as starting chain.
Row 1: Sc 1 in second st from hook, 9 sc = 10 sc. From here on, ch 1 at the end of each row and turn work.
Row 2–8: Sc 2 in first st and 1 sc in each st = 17 sts.
Row 10: Sc2tog, 13 sc, and sc2tog = 15 sc.
Row 11: Sc2tog, 11 sc, and sc2tog = 13 sc.
Row 12: Sc2tog, 9 sc, and sc2tog = 11 sc.
Row 13: Sc2tog, 7 sc, and sc2tog = 9 sc.
Row 14: Sc2tog, 5 sc, and sc2tog = 7 sc.
Row 15: Sc3tog, 1 sc, and sc3tog = 3 sc.
Row 16: Sc3tog.

EYES

Wrap white yarn once around finger and then work 7 sc onto the resulting loop. Work round in a spiral, moving directly to the next row.
Rnd 1: 2 sc in each st = 14 sc.
Rnd 2: *Sc 1, 2 sc in next st*, repeat 7 times = 21 sc. Change to gray yarn.
Rnd 4: Work from back edge of preceding row sts. Sc 2, 1 hdc, 2 hdc in next sts, 1 dc, 2 dc in next st, 2 tr, 1 tr and 1 dc in next st, 1 dc, 2 dc in next st, 2 hdc in next st, 2 hdc, 2 sc, and 2 slip st. Fasten off. Crochet another similar piece.
Pupils: Wrap black yarn once around finger and then work 7 sc onto the resulting loop. Close circle with 1 slip st and cut yarn. Crochet other pupil similarly. Attach pupils to eyes.

EYEBROWS

Chain 15 in red as starting chain.
Row 1: Sc 1 in second st from hook, 13 sc = 14 sc. Ch 1 and 14 sc. Turn work and slip st 1 row. Fasten off. Crochet another eyebrow.

FINISHING

Sew backstitches across beak with doubled black yarn (see photo). Attach eyes and eyebrows. Make a little pom-pom out of yellow yarn and attach it to the top of the hat.

BLUE LIGHTNING PHONE PURSE

SIZE Approximately 8 x 12 cm
YARN Lightweight smooth blue, orange, and red.
CROCHET HOOK Size needed to obtain gauge.
OTHER MATERIALS Six white buttons for eyes .
STITCH PATTERN Crochet sc according to instructions.
GAUGE 18 single crochet = 10 cm.

BAG

Chain 24 in blue as starting chain and close ring with 1 sc in first ch. Work round in a spiral, moving directly to the next row. When work height is 11 cm, ch 110 for strap. Attach strap to opposite side of bag. Sc 1 row along top edge of bag to other side, from there directly on the carrying handle and then to the other upper edge. Steam pieces lightly.

→

BEAK

Wrap orange yarn once around finger, and sc 8 in ring. Continue working in a spiral, moving directly to the next row.

Rnd I: 1 sc in each st = 8 sc.

Rnd 2: Skip 1 st from previous rnd and sc into other sts = 7 sts.

Rnd 3: Skip 1 st from previous rnd and sc into other sts. Continue in this manner until 3 sts remain. Break yarn, slip through loops, and pull hole shut. Crochet two more identical pieces. Attach beaks to side of bag one above another. The topmost should be about 1 cm from top edge and the rest at about 2.5 cm intervals.

EYES

Chain 4 in red as starting chain and 7 dc in first st of chain. Fasten off.

Work 5 more identical pieces and attach them to either side of beaks with flat edge toward beak. Attach eye buttons above red patches.

TAIL FEATHERS

Chain 15 in black as starting chain and slip st 1 in 2nd st from hook. Slip st 3, 6 sc, and slip st 4 into chain. Fasten off. Work 2 more sets of tail feathers and attach to other side of bag in line with beaks.

PIGGY-PROOF TABLET CASE

SIZE Approximately 19 x 25 cm
YARN Lightweight smooth gray, black, and yellow.
CROCHET HOOK Size needed to obtain gauge and a smaller hook for eyes.
OTHER MATERIALS Two black buttons for eyes and a large black snap fastener, diameter 25 mm.
STICHES Crochet sc according to instructions.
GAUGE 13 sc with double strand yarn and larger hook = 10 cm.
NOTE Work case with double strand gray yarn.

With larger hook and double strand gray yarn, chain 48 as starting chain and close ring with slip st. Continue working in a spiral, moving directly to the next row. Sc until work height is 24 cm.

Change to double strand black yarn and work flat. Ch 1, turn, and 24 sc (one st in each st of previous row). Continue sc back and forth (flat) for 5 rows. From here on, ch 1 at the end of each row and turn work. Then begin decreasing at both edges. At the beginning of the row decrease 1 by sc2tog first 2 sts and at the end by sc2tog last 2 sts. Continue decreasing each row until 2 sts remain. Fasten off.

→

EYES

Work eye with white yarn and smaller hook.

Chain 7 as starting chain.

Row 1: Sc 1 in second st from hook, 5 sc = 6 sc. From here on, ch 1 at the end of each row and turn work.

Row 2: Sc 2 in first st, 4 sc, and 2 sc in last st = 8 sc.

Row 3-4: Sc 8.

Row 5: Immediately at beginning of row sc2tog, 4 sc, and sc2tog = 6 sc.

Row 6: Immediately at beginning of row sc2tog, 2 sc, and sc2tog = 4 sc.

Crochet other eye similarly.

BEAK

Beak crocheted with yellow yarn and smaller hook.

Crochet 2 chain stitches (ch) for starting chain.

Row 1: Sc 3 in 2nd ch from hook 3 = 3 sc. Ch 1 and turn.

Row 2: Sc 2 in first st, 1 sc, and 2 sc in last st = 5 sc. Ch 1 and turn.

Row 3-6: Sc 2 in first st and 1 sc in each st = 9 sc. Ch 1 and turn.

Row 7: 2 sc in first st, 8 sc = 10 sc. Ch 2 and turn.

Row 8: Sc in 2nd ch from hook (= increase) and 10 sc = 11 sc. Ch 2 and turn.

Row 9: Sc in 2nd ch from hook (= increase) and 11 sc = 12 sc. Ch 1 and turn.

Row 10-14: Sc2tog and sc in each st of previous row. Ch 1 and turn. Work now has 7 sts.

Row 15-16: Sc2tog at beginning and end of row. Ch 1 and turn. Sc3tog and fasten off.

FINISHING

Steam case lightly. Sew eyes onto flap using white yarn. Sew buttons to eyes. Attach beak to flap with black yarn using backstitches and then sew lines on beak for mouth as pictured. Attach large snap, one part on the bottom edge of the flap and the other lined up on the case.